portable
houses

portable houses

Irene Rawlings & Mary Abel

Gibbs Smith, Publisher

Salt Lake City

First Edition
08 07 06 05 04   5 4 3 2 1

Published by
Gibbs Smith, Publisher
P.O. Box 667
Layton, Utah 84041

Order toll-free: (1-800) 748-5439
www.gibbs-smith.com

Front cover design by Kurt Wahlner
Designed and produced by Loneta Showell
Printed and bound in Hong Kong

Library of Congress Cataloging-in-Publication Data

Rawlings, Irene.
    Portable houses / Irene Rawlings & Mary Abel. — 1st ed.
       p. cm.
    Includes bibliographical references.
    ISBN 1-58685-347-3
    1. Mobile homes. 2. Recreational vehicles. 3. Tents.   I. Abel,
Mary. II. Title.
  TH4819.M6R39 2004
  643'.2—dc22
                                                    2003027206

contents

moving right along

Portable houses are getting more attention today than they've had since the frontier closed. And this "new nomadism" concept calls for living small, taking advantage of new technologies, and being free to travel.

The idea of a portable house—of traveling while accompanied by our favorite possessions—is endlessly appealing. It starts when we are still children, listening with fascination to stories of pioneers living out of prairie schooners for months at a time while slowly making their way out West. That sense of adventure does not leave us when we become adults; it just intensifies. The portable houses of today have to be cozy and warm, but they also have to be practical. They must fit with our idea of simplifying our lives, of living lightly on the land, yet must have a technological component. We may want to travel small, but we also want our favorite creature comforts—radio, CD, wireless Internet access, and portable GPS.

Folks who enjoy living on the move cut across a broad spectrum—from young people just getting started to retirees following the sun. The portable houses they choose to call home cut across an equally broad spectrum—from old steel shipping containers to shiny Boeing jets, from vintage trailers to new RVs, from tents, tepees, and yurts to floating homes, from remodeled sheep wagons to restored train cars.

From left: A yurt is strong, durable, and able to handle snow loads up to 232 psf and wind loads of 125 mph; the architectural grade fabrics for the roofs and walls are able to withstand harsh conditions, and the interior resembles a posh retreat. This restored Spartan trailer, updated with air conditioning and a new kitchen, is used by Rob and Maria Sinskey to travel from their home in California's Napa Valley to organic farms along the Oregon coast.

While traveling around the country putting together this book, we met so many people who wanted to share their portable home ideas with us. One young architect, Mike Latham, designed a six-foot-square steel-and-acrylic box with a bed on top and storage below. Randy Carlson, who restores Volkswagen campers to their original condition, said, "They have such a great demeanor, and they make you take a little more time with your travels." Jay Shafer, an art professor at the University of Iowa, built a tiny, charming Victorian home on wheels. It cost $42,000 to build and used only 4,800 pounds of building materials. Page Hodel learned plumbing and carpentry from do-it-yourself books in order to turn a 1972 International Harvester school bus into a comfortable home.

Jennifer Siegal, associate professor of architecture at Woodbury University in Los Angeles and principal of Office of Mobile Design, has watched this trend develop over the past few years. She says, "You're not bound or rooted to place. It's an idea that goes back to nomads through history. I see our society responding quite well to that due to new technologies, the global economy, and other such factors." Throughout her career she has focused on various aspects of mobile architecture, designing several 40-x-12-foot mobile structures using packing crates and retired shipping containers.

From left: A wood-sided tent, designed by Stephanie Sandston, turns a common-man's wall tent into a classy, more permanent structure. It requires little maintenance beyond knocking snow off the roof, and can be easily disassembled and moved to a new location. The term *gypsy wagon* has such a romantic connotation. This one, remodeled by Lynn Arambel, is decorated in warm, luxurious fabrics and has all the comforts of home, including a pillow that reads "There's no place like home."

trailers

The golden age of trailer travel, from the 1930s to the 1960s, was a time when Americans found it easier than ever to get away from it all while taking all the comforts of home with them. The family vacation combined the adventure (and economy) of camping with not having to really "rough it." Not a sleeping bag, a bed. Not a campfire, a propane stove. Families enjoyed visits to exotic places like New Mexico, South Dakota, or California without leaving the comfortable and familiar behind. It is always good to meet a new geography while not having entirely left the old one.

During the past four decades, people began traveling almost exclusively by plane, over-flying the national parks and roadside attractions that were part of their childhood memories. At the same time, motor campers became more utilitarian but less interesting as wood and aluminum gave way to plastic and vinyl.

Now baby boomers—the children who climbed into the back of the station wagon pulling the family's Airstream on a cross-country adventure—are rescuing these relics from fields, streams, and farms. They are finding vintage trailers through want ads, in junkyards and on the Internet. They are restoring them to their original glory and creating comfortable spaces in which to make new travel memories. Recent surveys show that Americans are traveling closer to home, regardless of available vacation time or money. They are taking classic American vacations to explore our national parks and forests or to camp at the lake or in the mountains. By pulling a few of their favorite things behind them in a renovated trailer, today's families can enjoy that thrill of the open road as their parents or grandparents did. And you can, too.

Sisters on the Fly plan trips all over the West to fish, play poker, tell tall tales, and enjoy being cowgirls. Each of the trailers has a name and a theme. Debra's trailer is a 1962 Kencraft called Annie Lee Rose. Maurrie's trailer is a 1969 Scotsman called Madame X—one of the flies she uses on the Madison River.

sisters on the fly

MODEL: 1969 Scotsman
SIZE: 120 square feet
OWNER: Maurrie Sussman
HOME BASE: Phoenix, Arizona

MODEL: 1962 Kencraft
SIZE: 160 square feet
OWNER: Debra Bolnick
HOME BASE: Bozeman, Montana

*m*aurrie Sussman started remodeling trailers about five years ago. Although she has remodeled more than thirty trailers for herself, for friends, and for women who have since become friends, she still has her first trailer—a 1958 Holiday called Lucy. "She was trashed when I first saw her," she says, "but when I walked inside . . . it was instant love."

It can take up to a year to restore a trailer if you're doing all the work yourself. But Maurrie is not all work and no play. She's formed a group called "Sisters on the Fly," women who have restored trailers and meet every few months in predesignated locations throughout the West to fish, eat, play poker for pennies, share tips about trailer remodeling, and tell stories about whatever else comes to mind while they relax around a campfire.

Maurrie looks for trailers from the 1950s and 1960s because they are still affordable and have "good bones," but she makes sure the frame is structurally sound. "It is difficult and costly to fix the twisted frame of a trailer that has blown over," she says. "I also try not to buy anything with the tin peeling off or with broken axles." She goes on to say that, if you really love the trailer, even axle problems can be fixed efficiently and not too expensively if they are discovered early in the remodeling process. To fix or replace peeling tin, however, can be quite expensive.

The first thing Maurrie does when she acquires a trailer is to scrub down every inch of the inside and outside. "As I clean, my

"How do you know when you're finished decorating?

Hook your trailer up and take it for a ride.

Everything that ends up on the floor is too much."

Once you name your trailer and choose a theme—
cowgirl, Americana, vintage '50s, rock and roll—
decorating becomes easy and fun.

hands touch and get to know every square inch of my trailer," she says. "This way, I get a feel for what's broken and what needs to be fixed."

Then she takes out the propane lines because they are often dangerously corroded. She replaces only the lines to the stove, not to the heater. "There are so many things that can go wrong with a propane heater, so I use a featherbed for warmth at night." On the cooking question, she cautions that unless your trailer is unusually well ventilated the smell of cooking can linger unpleasantly long.

Ripping out the old floors or covering the old linoleum floors is the next step. You can use new wood flooring or the once-again popular sheet linoleum—not to be confused with vinyl flooring. Vinyl is a synthetic product made of chlorinated petrochemicals. Linoleum, regarded as a "green" flooring, is produced from all-natural ingredients—oxidized linseed oil, cork dust, wood flour, tree resins, and pigments on a jute backing. While most vinyl patterns are printed onto the surface, linoleum's colors go all the way through, so as it wears, different layers of color are revealed. Linoleum is available in vibrant hues or in the vintage colors and patterns we remember from Grandma's kitchen.

The very next thing, according to Maurrie, is choosing a name. "When you name your trailer, the decorating all falls into place." Next Maurrie puts in new wood paneling and kitchen cabinets. Then she paints—both inside and out—and makes cushions, bed coverings, and curtains. "Make sure to line your curtains so they will look good from the outside."

The exteriors are then painted with larger-than-life portraits of cowgirls, recalling the "nose art" popular on World War II airplanes.

Decorating a small space is always a challenge. Maurrie suggests choosing a single color combination and sticking with it throughout the entire trailer. Visual interest comes with artistically layering the different patterns and textures.

Debra Bolnick (left) and her daughter play cards outside her trailer, Annie Lee Rose. Some other "Sisters on the Fly" trailers are named Sister Sioux, Rhinestone Cowgirl, Calamity Jane, Maudie Mae, Mustang Sally, Vacarra Guerra, and Zelda.

You can do this yourself if you are artistically inclined or find a local sign painter who enjoys doing caricatures.

WHAT TO LOOK FOR Walk around inside. Sit down. Either you love it or you don't. It's that simple. The great models are Scotsman, Fireball, Holiday, and Cardinal from the 1950s; Oasis, Golden and Play-mor from the 1960s; Fleetwing from the 1970s.

WHAT TO AVOID Stay away from any trailer that has been rain damaged. The "bones" are made from wood strips, so if it has rotted you'll have to rebuild the entire trailer.

Try not to fall in love with a trailer that's been flipped—that is, blown over in the wind—because the frame is very likely to have been bent. Telltale signs are deep scratches, dents, and gashes concentrated on one side of the trailer. Straightening a bent frame is expensive. Peeling tin and broken axles can also be expensive to fix.

WHAT IT'S GOING TO COST Vintage trailers can cost from $200 to $1,500. Ones with all the original parts are the most desirable and most expensive. If it doesn't have any structural damage, remodeling will run between $4,000 and $8,000.

REMODELING Take everything out and scrub down the trailer. After your trailer is clean, give it a name. Once it has an identity, it will be easy for you to rebuild and redecorate. Don't restore to perfection. Fix what can be fixed and paint and wallpaper; put fabric over the rest.

ON THE ROAD Vintage trailers were originally made to be pulled along the highway by the family car. However, cars in the 1950s were heavier and had 6- or 8-cylinder engines. Today's cars are lighter and not particularly well designed for towing. To comfortably haul a trailer, you'll need a half-ton SUV or truck with a minimum of 200 horsepower.

family, friends & food

MODEL: 1946 Spartan Manors
SIZE: 256 square feet
OWNERS: Rob and Maria Sinskey
HOME BASE: Napa, California

Traveling with friends Launce and Amanda Gamble and their children, Gus and Jane, the Sinskey caravan, *opposite*, finds a shady spot beneath the willows. High-quality bedding and linens, *above*, encourage a few quiet moments.

*f*or organic wine maker Rob Sinskey, chef and cookbook author Maria Sinskey, and their daughters Lexi and Ella, cruising across the country in one of their two 1946 Spartan Manor trailers is a true family vacation. With distractions like computers and televisions eliminated, the Sinskey family can discover the vast beauty of this country—and enjoy each other's company.

Rob hired former Hollywood set designer Craig Dorsey of Vintage Vacations to restore the two identical trailers in two different ways—both with a nostalgic nod to the 1940s. (Craig's website, www.vintage-vacations.com, is a great place for "trailerites" to communicate with each other and get restoration tips.) Craig scoured fabric stores and second-hand shops to find retro-style fabrics and accessories to create these cozy and comfortable homes away from home.

The interior originally consisted of an observation area in the front, gallery in the middle, and bedroom in the back. Rob converted the observation area into a wraparound kitchen, complete with a dinette table that can be converted into a bed. Although the kitchen is small, it has a stove with four burners, an oven that fits a full-sized cookie sheet on each of its two racks, and a three-way (AC, DC, and propane) refrigerator. French net shopping bags hang from the ceiling holding fresh fruits and vegetables—"food and decor all in one," says Maria.

Because of aircraft ingenuity (Spartans were originally designed by J.P. Getty and built by the Spartan Aircraft Company), they are strong yet incredibly lightweight. To haul the trailers, Rob uses a Ford F250 diesel truck "sturdy enough that when we are coming down mountains we won't be pushed down by the trailer." Since braking is an important issue when pulling something so big, Rob equipped the trailers with independent electronic brakes.

WHAT TO LOOK FOR Think "safety first" when shopping for Spartans: look for a solid frame and know that more often than not you'll have to replace the axle. Do this first, as it is relatively inexpensive to replace if done at the beginning of the restoration process.

WHAT TO AVOID Spartans are basically "tin cans," susceptible to condensation. Watch for condensation/water damage, which causes mold and mildew. Also keep an eye out for extensive body damage—Rob's had a small dent in the side that was easily repaired.

WHAT IT'S GOING TO COST The Sinskeys paid $3,500 for their yellow-and-red Spartan and $8,500 for the silver one, which had all the original equipment. Costs for restoration will vary, depending on how much work you do yourself and the extent to which you are committed to historical accuracy. Rob says he spent approximately $40,000 to restore his first trailer and a "budget-blowing" $100,000 to finish the silver Spartan.

REMODELING TIPS Again, Rob's motto is "safety first." He removed the floor furnace and had the stove and heat converted to propane. He also installed carbon monoxide and carbon dioxide detectors. For lighting, Rob chose a solar-panel 12-volt system. Because trailers are such a contained space, Rob suggests using natural finishes, such as AURO waxes and wood finishes, to eliminate off-gassing from finishes like lacquer.

Right: Ella Sinskey, relaxes on the sofa, covered with a nostalgic bark cloth. The surrounding woodwork is finished with German-made, all-natural AURO furniture wax. The range, *far right,* is deeper than it is wide and has four burners.

Opposite: Maria Sinskey helps the children prepare tasty treats from the organic food they collect on their travels, "Kids are more apt to try 'weird' food if they are involved in the cooking process."

The well-known MacKenzie-Childs look is infused into Victoria and Richard's 1966 Airstream. So many layers of bold color and pattern may not be for everyone, but the idea is to create a space that reflects the style and personality of its owner.

fabergé airstream

MODEL: 1966 Airstream
SIZE: 240 square feet
OWNERS: Victoria and Richard MacKenzie-Childs
HOME BASE: Aurora, New York

anyone at all familiar with the charming, whimsical stylings of Victoria and Richard MacKenzie-Childs' line of enamelware, furnishings, and home accessories won't be a bit surprised by the luscious, pattern-filled interior of their 1966 Airstream. It is simply an extension of their belief that a home should be a mirror of its owner's personality.

Victoria found the shiny aluminum trailer up on blocks along the road in upstate New York. "I saw the trailer with a 'For Sale' sign at a nearby farmhouse. I bought it, dragged it home, hid it in the woods, and sent Richard on a treasure hunt as a birthday surprise."

Although Richard was thrilled with his present, he and Victoria had no idea how much work would be required to repair it. They parked it near the lake on their property and used it as a changing room or a place to escape with "a pot of tea." But when the time came to spruce it up, Victoria and Richard went with the style they are known for—turning the trailer into a "Fabergé egg that is opened up to find an amazing jeweled surprise inside."

Initially, the trailer was completely gutted and everything was replaced, from plumbing to electricity to cabinetry. Victoria enlisted the help of experienced local tradesmen and craftspeople to make sure these projects were done correctly, then began embellishing the interior in pattern upon pattern that is the MacKenzie-Childs signature style.

Some of the walls are an elaborate combination of seashells, beads, buttons, and colorful Indian corn. Grouting putty was used to hold the items in place.

Fun wall treatments are found throughout the trailer. Items such as seashells, beads, buttons, and Indian corn are adhered to walls with grouting putty. Because the putty sets up slowly, Victoria used nails and tape to help keep the keep the objects in place. "I was inspired by the incredible Corn Palace in Mitchell, South Dakota," she says.

The floor in the galley kitchen is made of patterned tin, held in place with brass and copper upholstery tacks. The floors in the rest of the trailer are vintage linoleum Victoria found under the carpet in their home. She papered the inside of an armoire with old *National Geographic* covers and decoupaged the bathroom door with photos taken on family trips. She tiled the bathroom (relocated to the aft of the trailer) with soft and opaque lake glass and lake brick. The toilet is disguised as a rattan chair.

Finally, souvenirs from travels were placed throughout the trailer. "After all," says Victoria, "what else would you do with these things except put them into a traveling home?"

WHAT TO LOOK FOR Buy a trailer that is structurally sound and roadworthy. You're going to have enough work refurbishing it without worrying about whether it is going to stand up or fall down.

WHAT TO AVOID Rot, rats, and mildew.

WHAT IT'S GOING TO COST The sky is the limit. Victoria hired craftspeople to do the building and carpentry but did all the decorating herself by using found objects, fabric remnants, emptying her button box, and beachcombing the shores of Finger Lakes in upstate New York for lake glass and lake brick.

REMODELING TIPS Create a space you will love. Be bold. This is not your primary home, so do something different—something wild. Think color. Don't be afraid to experiment. Recycle. Use your imagination to find new uses for old objects. To separate the galley and the dining area, Victoria made a beaded curtain out of old wooden spools of silk thread. "The thread is too old and brittle to use for sewing, but when it catches the light, it is still so gorgeous."

The sleek, simple stylings of this Airstream trailer, *opposite*, show no signs of the elaborate design inside. "It's like a Fabergé egg that is opened up to find an amazing jeweled surprise inside," says Victoria MacKenzie-Childs. A vintage car and chauffeur wait to take the trailer on an adventure.

The interior, *below*, is a dazzle of color, pattern, and texture. The table is set with MacKenzie-Childs tableware. The trompe l'oeil painting on the walls mimics the lakeside view outside.

copper creek trailer

MODEL: 1956 Terry trailer
SIZE: 78 square feet
OWNERS: Hilary Heminway and Terry Baird
HOME BASE: McCloud, Montana

*t*he charming, teardrop shape of this small Terry trailer first charmed business partners Hilary Heminway and Terry Baird. Because it was in rough condition, Terry disassembled it down to the floor, took measurements, and rebuilt it to the same size and shape—only heavier and stronger. He used 1-1/8-inch plywood for the frame, stiffened the tongue with angle braces, put in a heavy-duty axle and two new tires. A local tinsmith cut 3 x 10-foot sheets of copper for the siding. "We used the old aluminum siding as a pattern . . . something like using a paper pattern to make a dress," says Terry. The copper was attached to the new plywood frame with brass screws (copper is too soft for screws) to mimic the rivets in the old aluminum trailer. "Copper ages well in the West and acquires a nice greenish-gold patina," says Hilary, who designed the interior of the trailer. Her challenge was to create a uniquely Western woodsy look while keeping everything in scale and leaving the interior space as uncluttered as possible.

WHAT TO LOOK FOR Are you going to pull it with your car or do you have a pickup? That will determine the size and weight of the trailer you should buy. Will you be doing the work yourself? You can buy a trailer in "rougher" shape and still keep restoration costs down.
WHAT TO AVOID Any trailer that's had a leaky roof (the interior plywood will be stained and possibly delaminated). Look at the tires and avoid a trailer that has twisted tires and rims.
WHAT IT'S GOING TO COST In Montana, its perfectly fine to knock on someone's door if you see an older trailer sitting out in the yard. The cost can be from $50-$500. Another good source is an RV dealer who may have taken a vintage trailer in trade. The cost to take this trailer down to its frame, completely rebuild it, apply the copper siding, and redecorate it was nearly $35,000.

To hide the trailer's insulation, Hilary covered the ceiling with soft, sueded deer hide, *left.* The flooring is recycled wood; the walls are fir bead board. The banquettes are a pale gray-green leather with purple trim for an updated '50s look. Vintage cooking pots hang above a copper-covered wood counter. A two-burner gas stove has been put into the counter.

The little cedar windows, *right,* have copper screens and are framed with lodgepole pine for a whimsical, western look.

buses & RVs

In the last few years, Americans have found a renewed interest in traveling closer to home, exploring and enjoying the blue highways of the United States, Canada, and Mexico. RV sales have reflected that sentiment: consumer demand for RVs has increased steadily over the past two years and RV shipments in 2004 are expected to reach their second-highest level in twenty-six years. Those who are already living the RV lifestyle have a freedom not possible with an airplane or in a hotel room—to go where they want and when they want at their own speed.

The popularity of RV travel hasn't been lost on land developers, either. Luxury RV "resorts" are popping up across the country, some with amenities like golf courses, spas, private Jacuzzis, and Internet hookups.

When talking about portable lifestyles, the first images that come to mind seem to be the big "land yachts"—luxurious motor homes like the ones in which country-western singers travel from town to town, bringing with them everything they need to create comfort and a sense of home. But there's more to the mobile-home scene than big RVs. We take a peek inside a refurbished school bus and learn all the dos and don'ts of making such a bus your home. We also talk with a man whose life's work is reconditioning vintage Volkswagens. He tells us what to look for and what to avoid when buying those amazingly long-lived bugs and campers.

Buses, campers, and RVs—comfortable, livable spaces that offer tons of amenities without sacrificing an ounce of personal style.

ROXANNE
ROXANNE

Owner Page Hodel discovered this 1972 school bus for sale on the side
of the road. She bought it, gutted it, insulated it, and made it her home.

roxanne roxanne

MODEL: 1972 International Harvester
SIZE: 320 square feet
OWNER: Page Hodel
HOME BASE: Sonoma County, California

Page Hodel wasn't looking for a bus that fine autumn day in 1986 when she took a drive in California's wine country . . . but a bus found her. "I saw a bus by the side of the road with a 'for sale' sign on it," she says. "It whistled at me and said 'Here I am.' I stopped, peeked in through the dirty windows, and was totally hooked."

The first challenge was finding a place to park it while she worked on it. After looking at every boatyard and steelyard in the ship-building area on San Francisco's waterfront, she found a boatyard that charged her $75 a month. She started work by ripping out the seats and stripping it down so it was an open space. Then she had a bus-warming and bus-naming party. The name Roxanne Roxanne, inspired by pioneer female rapper Roxanne Shante's 1987 hit single, "Roxanne's Revenge," was chosen because, as Page says, "Shante was sassy, naughty, and fierce, and I'm a gypsy at heart and admired all of that."

Then she built a floor ("a nice floor with insulation") and started imagining room configurations for the interior of her new home. To help her visualize, she took masking tape and marked out the various rooms—a living room, a kitchen, a bedroom, and a bath. "It was a fluid process," she says, "like doing a sculpture." She wanted her rooms to flow into each other "like in a real home"; she didn't want the rooms to "open off a hallway on one side like a lot of RVs seem to do."

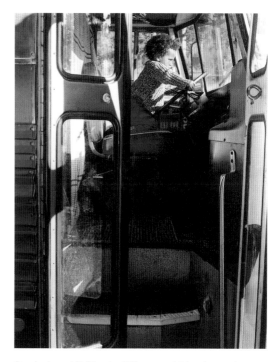

Page's niece, Lili Chartier-DiJiacomo, thinks about taking a little drive. Roxanne Roxanne still has her original International Harvester engine, which is simple to run and easy to fix.

"I saw a bus by the side of the road with a 'for sale' sign on it. It whistled at me and said, 'Here I am.' I stopped, peeked in through the dirty windows, and was totally hooked."

A nautical mirror, *top*, is one of Page's favorite things. The bedroom's built-in TV and VCR, *above*, compete with the view outside. Page and a friend, *opposite*, relax over a simple breakfast.

Page framed the interior of her bus with 1-x-2-inch Douglas fir, used 3/8-inch flexible plywood as the skin for the walls, and put redwood paneling (tongue-and-groove slats) over the plywood. She constructed the curved cupboards out of high-end birch plywood paneling. "I was going to make square corners, but the rounded edges just seemed so perfect."

When she started her bus project, Page didn't know the first thing about carpentry or plumbing, but she learned fast. "I bought the entire series of Time-Life and Sunset do-it-yourself books on wiring, plumbing, and carpentry and I followed the directions to the letter," she says.

The books couldn't help her with challenges peculiar to restoring a bus, however. After the fact, she discovered that she had located her toilet directly over the driveshaft. "Ideally you'd want the drain pipe to go straight down into a tank," she says, "but I had to give that pipe a wee little bend." Another mistake was hammering the plywood interior right into the main wiring harness and shorting out all the electrical systems. "It helps to know what's behind the walls of your bus," she says. "It would have been easy enough to get some schematic drawings . . . you can probably get them on the Web."

Her shipshape little bathroom (6 x 8 feet) has a toilet, a tiny sink she made by drilling a drain hole in a mixing bowl ("I broke several before I was successful") and a large soaking tub. The small, homey kitchen (8 x 8 feet) has a four-burner propane stove, a refrigerator, a stainless-steel sink, plenty of cupboards, and specially constructed shelves with "little restrainers" so the glass jars and canisters don't fall and break when the bus is in motion. The living room (10 x 8 feet) is dominated by a large, comfortable sofa. "I had no idea it was so big until I got it into the bus," says Page.

Page installed all the plumbing in the kitchen, *above*, using Time-Life
do-it-yourself books as a reference. A propane stove, small sink,
and a bit of counter space add up to a tiny but functional kitchen.

WHAT TO LOOK FOR Find a bus that is watertight. Do a thorough check of the outside skin, especially the seams and the joints on the roof—anywhere metal meets metal and is joined together.

Look for a bus that has not been customized too much so you can do your own remodeling work. Also, if the engine is original and your bus breaks down anywhere in the country, it can be fixed by a local school-bus mechanic.

WHAT TO AVOID Rust is your biggest enemy since it could cause your portable home to collapse on the freeway. Check the floor panels and the underside of the bus for any signs of rust.

WHAT IT'S GOING TO COST $5,000 to $10,000 for a clean and rust-free old-style school bus with a gasoline engine; $60,000 or more for a retired diesel Greyhound or Trailways bus, depending on condition.

REMODELING Spend enough time under the bus to get a good idea where the driveshaft, axles, and gas tank are. Try not to interfere with these "structural elements" when you are designing the interior. You can get mechanical and electrical schematics on the Web at www.busnut.com. Sit down with a pot of coffee or a glass of wine and decide where you want the rooms to be . . . or whether you want your bus to be one large loft-type space. Visualize how you want to live.

Rip out all the seats and everything that is not part of the body. Page's only regret is that she didn't keep the old hand-crank door opener.

Think about the identity of the bus as your new home. Use masking tape to define the rooms. Keep moving the tape until you have the configuration you want. Making the changes up front will keep you from making costly mistakes during construction.

Measure all the furniture you want to put into the bus to make sure it will fit and be in proportion. Remember, there isn't just one "right way" to remodel a bus.

ON THE ROAD Roxanne Roxanne still has her original International Harvester engine (simple to run and easy to fix). She gets 13-15 miles per gallon on the road, 10-13 miles in the city.

Roxanne Roxanne takes a little break along the side of a country road. Page calls the renovation "a fluid process . . . like doing a sculpture."

snug bug

MODEL: 1967 Volkswagen Westfalia
SIZE: 50 square feet
OWNERS: Randy and Vanessa Carlson
HOME BASE: Brea, California

One very good reason to buy an old Volkswagen camper and go cruising in it . . . is to slow yourself down," says Randy Carlson, who owns and restores old Volkswagens—both campers and bugs. This slower pace allows Randy and his family to take more time getting to their destination and to see more out the windows. "You get in it, motor along, and the world goes by you and you just let it go . . . it's the Zen of the trip." Randy has had a love affair with Volkswagen campers since the 1980s. His dream is to find a car that has all the service records "back to day one" because "an owner who saves all the receipts is probably taking good care of the car."

When Randy first buys a vintage car, he likes to just sit in it and say, "Isn't this thing cool?" Then he makes a big old list of things that have to be done. Some people do the mechanical work first, but Randy likes to do the cosmetics first, so he removes all the trim from the camper and takes it to a paint and body shop. "I always do the pretty stuff first because it motivates me to do the ugly (mechanical) stuff," he says. "I want it to run as good as it looks." As a general rule, Randy paints his campers their original color because that gives them resale value. "Original colors and original equipment are always the best choice."

WHAT TO LOOK FOR A Volkswagen camper with a solid, rust-free body and one that has not had any serious body damage. Find a car that has been driven in a dry climate like California, Arizona, New Mexico, or Nevada. The most desirable models are the split-windshield campers from 1967 and earlier. The 1968-1971 models are next on any collector's list. The 1971 was the last year to have the upright 1600 engine (cheap and easy to maintain) and the first to have front disc brakes.

WHAT TO AVOID Old Volkswagens, especially those from the East Coast and the Midwest, that have rust. Look for bubbling and rust at the very bottom forward edge, in the wheel wells, and on the floor.

WHAT IT'S GOING TO COST Unrestored camper 1955-1967—$4,000-$7,000; 1968-1979—$2,000-$4,000. Restored camper 1955-1967—$9,000-$15,000; 1968-1979—$7,000-$10,000. An average home-done restoration (not counting labor) may cost $3,000-$5,000. A professional restoration will run $5,000-$10,000, depending on the condition of the camper prior to restoration.

Originally, the upholstery would have been green to match the body color, but Randy thought he'd have a little fun with the interior of his camper. He chose a basket-weave vinyl material, similar to that originally used by Volkswagen, but in a bright red fabric. To add even more of a homey touch, his wife, Vanessa, made red gingham curtains for the windows. She also made gingham tablecloths and napkins to match.

rock-'n'-roll bus

MODEL: Prevost H3-45 body/ Ventaro conversion
SIZE: 357 square feet
OWNER: Tom Martino
HOME BASE: Denver, Colorado

*t*he body and mechanicals of this bus were built in the Prevost bus factory and then sent to Ventaro to be converted. Although there are a host of smaller companies, there are three major converters—Ventaro, Marathon, and Liberty—that transform bus chassis into year-round luxury motor homes. Standard equipment is central, generator-powered heat and air conditioning, central stereo system, multiple TVs (with a tracking satellite), cook-top stove, microwave, and washer/dryer.

Although there are many decorating options, Tom Martino advises designing the interior in classic earthtones with the "flair" coming from pillows and other accessories. "Keep the walls, cabinets, countertops, floor, and couches neutral," says Tom. "That way you aren't limited by passing fads. Believe me, taking out one of those couches is a great deal of work."

WHAT TO LOOK FOR Have a qualified bus mechanic look at the motor chassis, clutch, tires, and transmission. Check for leaks in the plumbing and air-conditioning systems. Pressurize the systems to make sure the pumps are running properly.

WHAT TO AVOID Water damage will destroy the value of your coach. Check the roof/ceiling where antennas or satellite dishes have been attached. These are the places most likely to leak.

WHAT IT'S GOING TO COST Only about 300 coach conversions are sold annually in the U.S. and they cost between $800,000 and $1.3 million. A used coach from the early 1990s can cost $200,000-$750,000, depending on age and condition.

ON THE ROAD Most new coaches are powered by Detroit Diesel series 60 engines, which is good because every repair shop has the parts and every bus mechanic knows how to work on them. The older Detroit Diesels are reliable but can burn a lot of oil. Caterpillar and Cummins Diesel engines are also very reliable. For mountain driving, 470 HP gets by, but 500 HP is optimal.

The Stlendive (also available as AEG/Zanussi) washer/dryer, *above*, is a unique one-step system. After the final spin, this front-loading washer turns into a dryer. The exterior of the bus, *below*, is a giant canvas for artistic expression.

trains,
planes & boats

Trains have always had an aura of mystery, intrigue, and romance about them. Perhaps that's because train travel evokes a slower, more elegant time when well-dressed ladies and gentlemen took journeys instead of trips. White-gloved waiters served meals on white table linens with real china and silver. Even now, train travel is a wonderful way to see the country without having to drive or stare at miles of interstate highway. Having a private car filled with all the comforts of home and hooking it up to the train is enough to fulfill all the wanderlust in your heart.

For those folks who love the water—be it a river, lake, or the ocean—the only thing more fun than paddling, motoring, or sailing is actually living right on the water. Folks have reconditioned everything from houseboats to tugboats, from old ferryboats to vintage yachts. The reasons are always the same and stated quite succinctly by River Rat in Kenneth Grahame's *The Wind in the Willows:* "There's nothing—absolutely nothing—half so much worth doing as simply messing about in boats." And there's nothing quite like the feeling of being rocked to sleep by gently lapping water.

Airplanes, on the other hand, are all about speed. Having your own plane conjures up words like *jet set.* Sleek and fast, private airplanes hurtle through the air whisking those with deep pockets effortlessly from city to city . . . without a strict timetable, without long waits at security checkpoints, or without a charge for extra baggage. A truly worry-free vacation.

Although most of us can't afford to live on a train car, on the water, or in the air, we can always enjoy a glimpse into the lifestyles of those who can.

caritas

MODEL: 1948 Pullman 14/4 Sleeper
SIZE: 850 square feet
OWNERS: Clark Johnson and Nona Hill
HOME BASE: Minneapolis, Minnesota

Caritas started life in 1948 as a four-bedroom, fourteen-roomette sleeper, operating on such famous trains as the Texas Special. By the time Clark Johnson bought her in 1964, she was a little "long in the tooth." He started remodeling by ripping out the fourteen roomettes (he kept the four 6 x 8-foot bedrooms) and replacing them with a galley, observation room, and a master bedroom with a shower. Caritas now sleeps eight passengers and a crew of two. The 10 x 5-foot platform at the rear of the car seats five people comfortably. "One of my greatest delights is sitting on the back platform with a martini and watching the world go by," says Clark.

WHAT TO LOOK FOR Do a walk-through with an Amtrak certified inspector. Some sage advice from Clark, who has spent twenty years and more than $250,000 remodeling and tinkering with Caritas: "Buy a car that someone else has already redone."

WHAT TO AVOID Rust—make sure the side sills that run the length of the car (at the floor) and carry the car's weight are not rusted. Check to make sure that the center sill (the beam that runs along the bottom of the car and couples one car to the next) is in good shape.

WHAT IT'S GOING TO COST $10,000 can buy a car in workable condition. A car that's certified to Amtrak's standards can cost $250,000 and up. An annual Amtrak inspection costs $600.

ON THE ROAD To hook up to a regularly scheduled Amtrak train costs $1.15 per mile. In Canada, ViaRail charges $2.00 per mile. Parking your train car on the siding costs between $100 and $200 per day (including water and electricity). There are approximately 150,000 miles of track in the U.S. and Amtrak runs on 22,000 of them. Explore off the beaten path. Get times and schedules from the quarterly Official Railroad Guide ($100).

Using the retired ocean liner *Queen Mary* as inspiration, Clark decorated the interior of his car, *above*, in an updated version of Art Deco.

Brightly colored Caritas, *opposite*, brings up the rear of a special train of private cars traveling as "The Kooteney Express" at Kooteney Landing near Nelson, B.C., Canada.

This bold decorating in such a confined space—the gold silk draperies, Murano glass chandelier, damask-upholstered antique seating, and plenty of books—gives this car the confident air of luxury. The 1928 Pullman Business Car was opulently decorated in the 1950s by writer and bon vivant Lucius Beebe and his friend Charles Clegg. Wade has painted and reupholstered everything at least once in the past twenty years but has stayed with the old Beebe-Clegg design.

virginia city

MODEL: 1928 Pullman Business Car
SIZE: 800 square feet
OWNERS: Wade and Julia Pellizzer
HOME BASE: Redwood City, California

When the opulently decorated train car once owned by well-known writer Lucius Beebe came up for sale, Wade Pellizzer jumped at the chance to buy it. "I've been interested in trains since I got one under the tree when I was a boy," he says. The three-bedroom (two have full-sized beds; one has bench seating during the day, upper and lower berths at night) car was in pretty good shape but needed a lot of mechanical work to bring it up to the current Amtrak safety specifications. "The specifications are updated annually; it is important to keep current," Wade adds.

WHAT TO LOOK FOR A good inspector (Amtrak has a list) can look for problems with the frame, sill, and mechanicals.

WHAT TO AVOID Most structural problems on Pullman cars come from age and rust. On Budd-Built cars (made out of stainless steel) check for metal-fatigue cracks in the frame.

WHAT IT'S GOING TO COST If the car is Amtrak certified, it will cost anywhere from $140,000 to $1.5 million. Twenty years ago, Wade bought Virginia City for $72,000. He has spent more than $250,000 bringing it up to current Amtrak specifications, installing a new generator and an Amtrak 480-volt electrical system. He has also repainted the exterior twice ($30,000). An exterior paint job usually lasts about fifteen years.

REMODELING Wade and Julia have repainted and reupholstered the furniture in the interior of the car "at least once" but have kept the original "posh 1950s" look.

ON THE ROAD Amtrak charges $1.15 per mile plus a terminal charge ($100-$200). When parking near a terminal, determine if the costs are in increments of days or hours. Costs per month to park the train can run up to $3,000 (includes insurance, parking fees, storage fee, and hook-ups).

The shiny blue Pullman car sits on the tracks at Union Station in Denver, Colorado, *above*. "Sleeping on a moving train is a great experience," says Wade. "For those of us who love it, the clack-clack of the wheels on the tracks is a lullaby."

jet set

MODEL: Boeing 737-500
SIZE: 120 square feet
DESIGNERS: Rob Lancaster/Greenpoint Technologies
HOME BASE: Seattle, Washington

designing the interior of an airplane is similar to designing an interior for anything else," says Rob Lancaster, who designed the interior of this Boeing 737. Similar? Well, if you overlook small differences like meeting FAA requirements—or bolting down everything from lamps to flower vases.

When starting a new project, Rob always asks the client to create a mission statement describing how he/she will use the space. Then together they come up with a deck plan and figure out which materials, fabrics, and wood veneers will be used. "I choose many of the materials based on their fire retardancy because fire is a big issue on an airplane," says Rob. He prefers working with natural fibers that have a lower flashpoint than synthetics. Another challenge is that all seating components must have seat belts and that floatation devices and life rafts need to be incorporated either under sofas, in cabinets, or in the ceiling of the aircraft.

After everything is done, an FAA inspector will do a "walk through" to make sure you followed your technical drawings to the letter.

Clean, contemporary furnishings, *opposite*, are a good fit for airplanes, which have strict safety standards and require that everything be bolted down. A simple but functional lavatory, *above*. A Boeing 737-500 portable house, *below*.

HOW TO BUY AN AIRPLANE For a new plane, go directly to the manufacturer. Used planes tend to be sold through brokers; some consumer magazines list business jets for sale.
WHAT TO LOOK FOR Age and flight hours. An airplane's age is determined by the number of flight hours on the airframe and how it is maintained. If a plane has been carefully maintained, the number of flight hours becomes less important.
WHAT IT'S GOING TO COST Used planes start at $250,000, depending on condition. Brand new? A cool $10-14 million.

The main cabin, one of the elegantly large spaces on *Trianon*, is crisply nautical in décor. Traditional furnishings include a comfortable upholstered sofa with coordinating chairs, an English coffee table, and ginger-jar lamps. Chromolithographs of boats of the 1940s and 1950s decorate the walls.

second time around

MODEL: 1960 Trumpy 83-foot cruiser
SIZE: 1,200 square feet
OWNERS: Jim & Susan Keenan
DESIGNER: Jack Fhillips Designs
HOME BASE: Palm Beach, Florida

Jim Keenan loves boats; especially, it seems, vintage wooden boats in need of a good (and expensive) overhaul. His love affair with *Trianon*, an 83-foot Trumpy cruiser, started more than twenty years ago, but he sold her in order to buy a larger boat. The story goes on: Many years later, he found her abandoned in a boatyard in a sorry state of sagging planks and cracking paint. "Trumpys are the survivors of another era—an era of elegant wooden boats," he says. "I decided that the second time around, I was going to restore her exactly as she was." He knew that restoration was a sentimental, expensive venture.

Built in 1960, *Trianon* was built of mahogany over white oak with durable teak railings and deck, but much of the wood was in bad shape. "One of the biggest challenges for someone who is considering the head-to-toe restoration of a boat that's been stored in the tropics is that all the woodwork is infested with bugs—termites and woodborers," says designer Jack Fhillips, who was brought on board to help direct the year-and-a-half restoration. "So the first project was to replace old lumber with new while still making it look old." To keep the problem from recurring, the boat is regularly dry-docked and fumigated.

While the boat was still "in pieces," new electrical wiring, a new air-conditioning system, and a state-of-the-art sound system were installed. The original engines were overhauled. Jack's design firm's next task was to research the history of Trumpy

The mahogany-and-teak exterior of *Trianon* follows the clean, classic look that designer Jack Fhillips describes as "how a classic gentleman would dress."

Yachts (one of America's foremost manufacturer of motor yachts from 1910 until 1973) and make sure that the interior design was correct. Unlike many contemporary luxury yachts, Trumpy living spaces are elegant and spacious while the sleeping berths are small. While designing, Jack considered integrity and suitability. "A lot of yachts have been tricked out to look like discos," he says. "My purpose was to re-create a classic yacht interior."

"This boat cried out to be done in blue and white," says Jack, a traditionalist designer. He continues to say that he pictured the boat "in terms of how a classic gentleman would dress." Jack used only natural fabrics—cottons, wools, and linens—because they withstand the sun and salt air better than synthetics and "because Trumpys were built before man-made fabrics were generally available." In addition to the specially made, comfortable upholstered couches and chairs, he chose antique accent pieces to reinforce the look *Trianon* would have had when first built.

WHAT TO LOOK FOR   Buying a classic boat is like buying a classic car. Buy something in the very best condition you can afford because you'll have less to fix. Have a thorough inspection done by an experienced wooden-boat restorer. Have the engine checked by a qualified marine mechanic.

WHAT TO AVOID   Wooden boats seem sturdy, but unless recaulked and repainted regularly, they can be a money pit. Avoid a boat that is bug-infested because you'll have to take it down to the skeleton. "If you don't have the patience or the money for an extensive restoration process, consider buying something new," says Jack.

WHAT IT'S GOING TO COST   Vintage wooden boats can cost from $200 to "the sky's the limit," depending on size and condition. Restored vintage Trumpys can cost between $400,000 and $800,000. If you buy a boat that needs restoration, buy something that's stable. Don't buy something that's cheap. Look for quality. Consider your wooden boat a sentimental investment that needs to be removed from the water at least once a year to be inspected, recaulked, and repainted.

The restoration of this 1960 Trumpy cruiser, *opposite*, was a labor of love for owner James Keenan, who owned her once, sold her, then found her abandoned. After purchasing her for a second time, James enlisted the help of designer Jack Fhillips to return her to her original beauty.

The aft of the 83-foot cruiser, *below*, is furnished with traditional teak, making it a perfect place for dinner alfresco.

tepees, tents & yurts

Most of us have childhood memories of tent-camping in the woods—as Boy Scouts and Girl Scouts, with church youth groups, or away for the first time at summer camp. Or, perhaps, we spent the summer reading James Fenimore Cooper's *The Last of the Mohicans* or *Leatherstocking Tales* and imagined ourselves as brave Uncas, creeping stealthily through the woods toward the camp of the Huron. Tents and tepees still bring us close to nature and near to the romance of our childhood memories.

The use of tents, tepees, and yurts—wonderfully ancient forms of shelter—by twenty-first-century travelers just goes to show that simplicity works: wood gives structure; canvas keeps out the elements. It's that simple. They are easy to make for the do-it-yourselfer (or you can buy one already made and furnished), easy to move, easy to maintain, and easy to enjoy. Today, the pioneering spirit that created these basic structures lives on as outdoor enthusiasts and environmentalists alike continue to find new uses for them—as guest rooms, kids' playhouses, home offices, writers' retreats, vacation homes, and, of course, portable houses.

Some of these fabric structures have been updated with contemporary synthetic materials and innovative designs; others have the same simple wood-and-cloth construction as they did hundreds of years ago. Some are loaded with modern-day conveniences like gas stoves, comfortable beds, and electricity; others are modestly furnished with a cot and a sleeping bag. However you define "roughing it," these structures fit the bill. Even so, many are outfitted with TV, cable, and Internet access—all necessary for living and communicating in the modern world.

This authentic reproduction of a Plains Indians tepee is luxuriously decorated with Western- and Adirondack-inspired furniture, Navajo rugs, and Indian artifacts. The cozy reading area includes a fringed horn-and-steer-hide chaise and an iron floor lamp with a painted rawhide shade.

rustic chic

MODEL: Authentic Bannock tepee
SIZE: 28-foot diameter/640 square feet
DESIGNER: Cassandra Lohr Design
HOME BASE: Aspen, Colorado

*t*he property has a pond surrounded with native grasses and cattails, a meadow full of wildflowers, aspen and evergreen trees, as well as a gorgeous view—a perfect spot for a tepee.

At first, creating and decorating a tepee may seem simple, but for people who are used to living in rooms with straight walls and angled corners, it poses a design challenge. "To begin with, a tepee is never totally round—it's egg-shaped," says Cassandra Lohr, who designed this tepee to be a study, writing space, and occasional guest room. This oval shape results from the tepee being canted slightly backward to allow for more headroom at the rear, the traditional living area, and an adequate space for the fire and air vent at the front.

All the larger pieces of furniture were specially designed with straight fronts and curved backs to conform to the shape of the tepee. "I wanted the pieces to have a rustic-chic look and to be historically correct to the late nineteenth- and early twentieth-century," says Cassandra. "All the antique pieces I found were, of course, square or rectangular in shape." Some of the pieces were designed to hide the technology necessary to modern life—including a pop-up cable TV and a complete office hidden inside a twig-embellished cabinet.

The structure itself is an authentic Bannock tepee but brought up to date with a lightweight, weather-resistant acrylic that lasts longer and is more waterproof than canvas. A semi-permanent wood floor lifts the tepee off the ground, keeping moisture and cold

Cassandra Lohr added the stone firepit for warmth and to maintain the authenticity of the Native American theme. The burled bed, hand-made by a Wyoming artisan, is covered by a Ralph Lauren fabric inspired by Beacon blankets.

You hear the wind blowing, the grasses rustling, and see some blue sky through the top. It's a peaceful place.

from seeping into the living space. The stone and curved-brick firepit (the only other part of the tepee that is not readily portable) is three feet deep and is designed so the smoke will vent through the opening at the very top. "The tepee's smoke flaps work pretty much like a flue on a fireplace," says Cassandra. "You close or open them to let air come in or smoke go out."

If you are not in the market for a designer-created-and-furnished tepee but you are reasonably handy, you can buy a tepee kit, modify it to suit your needs, and put it together in a few weeks. If you choose to make your tepee out of canvas, you can waterproof it with two coats of regular house paint.

WHAT IT'S GOING TO COST A custom tepee—designed and furnished—can cost upwards of $100,000. Manufactured tepee prices range from $500-$5,000, depending on size, fabric, and other features (such as chemical treatment with a fire-retardant or custom painting of Native American motifs on the outside). A tepee can be constructed as a do-it-yourself project, but you'll need a commercial sewing machine to handle the double or triple thickness of canvas. The poles (ideally lodgepole pine two to three inches in diameter) should extend four to five feet above the top of the canvas.

CHOOSING A LOCATION If you are putting your tepee up in a residential area, check your covenants for height restrictions. Tepees are often built with the entrance facing to the east— partly to capture the morning sun's warmth, partly to keep the westerly winds from filling the interior with smoke from the fire, and partly for traditional Native American religious reasons.

ON THE ROAD The fabric part of an average-sized tepee can be folded down to the size of a very large sleeping bag. You will need a pickup truck equipped with an extra-long rack for the tent poles, which range between a minimum of twenty-four feet (for a nineteen-foot-high tepee) and a maximum of thirty-six feet (for a thirty-foot-high tepee).

The Plains Indians erected their tepees near water for drinking and close to trees for shade. Today's tepee afficionado can simply choose the prettiest spot on their property—close enough to trees for shade but not close enough to be damaged by falling branches.

Basic creature comforts, such as a cot (covered with a feather bed, of course), a rustic table and chairs, real tableware and cloth napkins, and a vase of fresh flowers or pots of herbs, can create a sense of home even in the most barren landscape.

back to basics

MODEL: Miner's tent
SIZE: 80 square feet
OWNER: Sue Scott
HOME BASE: Marble Canyon, Arizona

*I*s there anything simpler or more basic than a canvas miner's tent?

Sue Scott was born and raised in Arizona and spent most of her life riding horses, camping out, and enjoying the magnificence of the American Southwest. She loves the Four Corners area, saying, "There's such a vastness, yet a deep sense of intimacy with the earth, when you're out in the middle of nowhere."

Although she tends to travel with only the bare necessities, there are a few items that she refuses to leave home without. "There are five things I always take on a trip," says Sue. They are, in no particular order, good pots, pans, and cooking utensils; real tableware, a tablecloth, and cloth napkins; good spices and a few cans of green chile; a battery-operated light; and a few of those books she's been meaning to read. "I always seem to drag along the same books," says Sue, "because the beautiful scenery keeps me from reading."

Sue also packs her tried-and-true flannel-lined down sleeping bag, her long johns, thick socks, and a ski cap. "And by all means, if the sky is beckoning, throw the horse blanket on the ground, drag your sleeping bag out of the tent, and sleep under the stars."

WHAT TO LOOK FOR An antique miner's or WW II army surplus canvas tent that is waterproof, stable, and easy to manage. When bugs and snakes are expected, make sure your tent has a sewn-in floor.
WHAT TO AVOID A tent that leaks. Hold it up to the light to detect any small holes. It will be heavy—ask a friend to help you.
WHAT IT'S GOING TO COST $20-$150.
ON THE ROAD Sue uses a mule team to pack it into remote locations. It's also possible to use an SUV or four-wheel drive vehicle.

Because she camps in such remote spots, Sue has her little luxuries—favorite books, sassy tin plates of her own design, bedding, even bunches of flowers—brought in by pack-mule train. She arrives at the campsite on horseback. "I could drive in an SUV, but I like to create a romantic, nostalgic atmosphere," she says.

Stephanie's tent is furnished with antiques acquired at local auctions. The chrome 1930s chair was originally in a barbershop in Butte, Montana. The 1950s leatherette-and-fabric armchair is a family piece. The bed coverings are vintage trade blankets, and wooden cross-country skis were a flea market find.

canvas cabin

MODEL: Hunter's "corn-crib" shack
SIZE: 336 square feet
OWNER: Stephanie Sandston
HOME BASE: Bozeman, Montana

Stephanie Sandston made her first hard-sided tent as a "fun space for my overflow of summer guests." She was inspired partly by the semi-permanent tents used by local hunters and partly by safari tents she saw in *National Geographic.* "Hard-sided tents just seemed more durable and more practical than ordinary tents—not exactly a tent and not quite a cabin," she says. Her own tents (there is more than one now) stay up in all seasons and need to have their canvas changed only every four to five years.

Does the canvas go on the inside of the wooden shell or on the outside? Stephanie has experimented with it both ways and found that her tents are more durable with the wood frame (she calls it corn cribbing) on the outside. "Horses and deer and even bear like to rub up against the tent and, eventually, they will wear out the canvas," she says. Of course, even hard-sided tents will not keep out a determined bear. "If they wanted to come in, they could," she says philosophically. "The trick is not to keep yummy food (other than coffee, which bears apparently don't like) in the tents overnight or when you are gone for the day—just hang it in a tree outside."

The tents are not insulated and rely on a small but efficient stove for warmth. "You have to remember to feed it, but it

keeps the tent warm even in sub-zero weather," she says. In summer, she opens the windows (copper screens keep out the bugs) and the front door to the Montana breezes. The lack of insulation allows a soft light to filter through the roof, making the tent seem larger than it really is.

Stephanie uses real canvas to make her tents. When asked about leaks, she says, "I expect to get some drips for the first couple of rains, then the canvas seems to 'tighten up' and it becomes completely waterproof."

The smallest tent Stephanie has made is 12 x 12 feet, and the largest 14 x 24 feet. The larger tent is designed to have a substantial front porch (12 x 6 feet) that can be open in good

Stephanie calls her hard-sided tent "a shack" and says it is "not exactly a tent but not quite a cabin."

weather and canvas-covered when it rains or snows. She says that 14 x 24 is about the largest she likes to build her tents. "It's better to cluster a number of them than to over-build." She has connected her hard-sided guest rooms with a wooden walkway.

Without plumbing, electricity, or heat (except for the stove), Stephanie's tents sit lightly on the land, require little maintenance, and can be easily disassembled and moved.

WHAT'S IT GOING TO COST To buy from Stephanie Sandston's Shack-Up: $20,000 for the 12 x 12, $25,000 for the 14 x 24, and $35,000 for a tent furnished with antique and vintage furniture. Do-if-yourselfers can buy the plans for $3,500. Stephanie puts in temporary footings and a floor, then she builds the outside like a corn crib. The fir boards are left rough on the outside and finished with linseed oil on the inside. They take about four weeks to complete.
ON THE ROAD The canvas folds up. The wood walls can be disassembled. You will need a long-bed pickup to transport this tent.

A very efficient hunting stove warms the entire space. The stove comes apart and can be packed out by horse. Behind the stove, a vintage porcelain-on-tin advertising sign keeps the tent's wooden walls from becoming too hot.

Yurts are an ancient form of shelter that have been modernized for today's nomads. They come in a variety of colors (green is the most popular because it blends in with the surrounding environment) and can be loaded with extras, such as wood-burning or gas stoves, French doors, insulated windows, and interior walls. Strong and durable, yurts can support up to 2,100 pounds of weight per square inch (such as snow) and stand up to sustained winds of over 100 miles per hour.

backcountry getaway

MAKER: Colorado Yurt Company
SIZE: 30-foot diameter/706 square feet
OWNERS: Dwayne and Lisa Raleigh
HOME BASE: Moab, Utah

*a*mazingly durable and portable, the yurt, a fabric-covered dwelling, was used by Mongolian tribes more than 2,500 years ago. When the flower children of the 1960s were looking for an inexpensive and portable way to live on the land, they brought this ancient structure into the twentieth century.

Today's yurts are made of vinyl laminate or a coated cotton/polyester blend and insulated with astro-foil (basically two layers of bubble wrap backed by aluminum foil) that reflects 85 percent of the heat back into the yurt. It also serves as insulation against the summer heat and acts as a vapor barrier.

Yurts can be set up directly on the ground or, for a more permanent structure (they are used as vacation homes, guest rooms, and even restaurants), they are assembled atop a wood deck. Easily broken down, the entire structure can be transported in the back of a standard pickup.

The big, open space of a yurt can be fun to decorate. Private spaces are created with "walls" of fabric, or some yurt companies sell interior partitions made of wood. Under the 14-foot-high roof, it's even possible to build a loft for sleeping.

WHAT TO LOOK FOR Chip Meneley of the Colorado Yurt Company suggests getting a yurt with plenty of windows (larger yurts can support up to ten). Also make sure you have enough insulation for the environment where you're setting it up.
BEFORE YOU BUY If you are considering a yurt as a guest room, check local zoning laws or neighborhood covenants.
WHAT IT'S GOING TO COST A 16-foot yurt costs $2,800 to $5,000; a 30-foot yurt costs $5,600-10,000. That doesn't include the cost of the deck.

The interior of this yurt is so comfortable there is little "roughing it."

sheep wagons

Sheep wagons came to the American West about 1884. There are many stories about just how the first sheep wagon came about, but the most plausible is that an Englishman came and settled in Wyoming where he saw Basque sheepherders sleeping out under the stars. Because there is a tradition of gypsy wagons and tinkers' caravans in the British Isles, he built similar wagons and sold them to the local sheep ranchers. In letters back home, the Basques described them as "baby prairie schooners."

The sheepherder, his dog, and his radio—it was a lonely existence. But the snug little wagon held everything a sheepherder needed while tending and protecting sheep from predators twenty-four hours a day in remote prairie pastures or mountain meadows. Although the shepherd supplied his own firewood and needed a good source of water, the wagon was, for the most part, self-contained. It had a big, comfortable bed, a stove, storage for clothing and cooking utensils, a pullout table that doubled as a writing desk, and a special shelf just above the bed for the radio.

Today, a growing number of people are captivated by the allure of the nomadic life. They are buying old gypsy wagons in Europe and having them shipped the the U.S. or restoring 100-year-old sheep wagons found at farm and ranch sales in Wyoming and Montana. Some, like artist Lynn Arambel, are building them from the ground up and turning them into livable works of art. Filled with good bedding and linens, antique accessories, and flea-market furnishings, these cozy, womb-like structures make unique guest rooms, gracious writing rooms, or quiet places in which to escape the hurried pace of the modern world—places that bring us back to simpler times and let us tune in to the sounds of nature.

american gypsy

MODEL: Modified ledge wagon
SIZE: 52 square feet
OWNER: Lynn Arambel
HOME BASE: Sheridan, Wyoming

an American gypsy wagon is built like a sheep wagon but instead of the traditional bow shape, the sides are splayed out at the top. This gives the wagon more wall space, more headroom, and allows for larger windows to give an airier feel.

For many years, Lynn Arambel has been restoring historic Wyoming sheep wagons for clients to use as guest rooms, writing studios, extra baths, and mother-in-law suites. She finally she decided to build something romantic just for herself. "I wanted a wagon that would appeal to a western woman—a cross between a gypsy look and a Virginia City look—with a beautiful saloon kind of feel . . . someplace for *Gunsmoke's* Miss Kitty to sleep," says Lynn.

Lynn researched ledge wagons in history books and on the Internet. She decided not to modify an existing wagon but to build her own original gypsy wagon. After designing the basic shape, she visited wheelwright Dave Engel of Engel's Coach in Joliett, Montana, to buy either new or reconditioned running gear from what he had in stock. "Dave is an incredible wagon restorer," says Lynn. "People bring buggies, farm wagons, stagecoaches, and even old horse-drawn ambulances to him for restoration, so I know I'm in good hands."

To make her gypsy wagon as traditionally western as possible, Lynn built the body of poplar, which is strong, light, and easy to work with. She started out with a basic sheep wagon shape, but when she got to the front benches (where the sheep wagon starts its traditional bread-loaf bow shape), she splayed out the

BE IT EVER
SO HUMBLE—THERE'S
NO PLACE
LIKE HOME

"Gypsies were natural collectors," says Lynn, "swapping for this, trading for that." With this in mind, she furnished her gypsy wagon with antique linens, elk-horn silverware, down pillows, and a linen duvet cover. There's even a little button-box accordion from the early 1800s.

A utilitarian yet lovely farmhouse sink occupies a corner of Lynn's gypsy wagon. Although she wanted to preserve a rustic look, the wagon has both plumbing and electricity. A vintage porcelain pitcher sits on the shelf over the sink.

top to give it a different look. The rafters were shaped out of 2 x 14-inch pieces of pine cut to the slightly arched roof design. Lynn strapped canvas over the top of the rafters, topped the canvas with an inch of fiberglass insulation, and attached a copper roof. She also created a little copper lip on the roof to carry the rain away from the body.

A 48 x 72-inch bed is covered with a collection of handmade blankets and shawls as well as down-filled throw pillows covered with antique fabrics. A table pulls out from underneath the bed to use as a writing desk or a place to eat. The wagon is electrified and has a hot plate for making tea or a pot of stew.

WHAT TO LOOK FOR A sturdy undercarriage. Make sure the running gear (wheels, bolsters, axles, skeins, reach, and brakes) is in good shape and the irons that support the wagon are not rusted.
WHAT TO AVOID A wagon with a rotted roof and/or a rotted floor—unless you are planning to rebuild the entire structure.
WHAT IT'S GOING TO COST Vintage gypsy wagons are only available in Europe and have to be imported at costs starting from $15,000 plus shipping. To build a gypsy wagon in the U.S. using new running gear (about $4,000) will cost around $14,000; using old and repaired running gear (about $1,500) will cost in the range of $11,500. A new gypsy wagon built on new running gear and appropriately furnished with antiques can cost upwards of $38,000.
REMODELING Scrub and disinfect the entire wagon. Seal and caulk seams to keep out dust, moisture, and mice. To reconstruct parts of the wagon, use poplar—it is light but sturdy.
ON THE ROAD If your wagon has the traditional wooden running gear, it will need to be pulled by a horse—a team of two horses if the tongue is a double tree. For a smoother ride, some people put rubber seals over the steel-banded wooden wheels.

bath house

MODEL: Tar-paper shack wagon
SIZE: 84 square feet
OWNER: Bee Young
HOME BASE: Brady, Texas

*t*his bath wagon may have started life as a "tar-paper shack wagon," used as sleeping quarters by road-building crews. Or maybe a nearby ranch needed another sheep wagon and banged together a quick, four-sides-straight-up structure. When it was found, the tar-paper walls had been covered with tin, effectively concealing the rotted wood structure inside. The wagon had to be rebuilt from the floor up, but, fortunately, the running gear was in good condition.

Bee Young wanted a bath house to put next to some sheep wagons she was using as guest rooms on her Texas ranch. She wanted an elegantly rustic room with a big claw-foot tub, antique sconces with crystal drops, and a country washbasin in the corner. She also wanted a big window that opened right in the back by the tub so she could settle in for a good soak while looking out on the wide Texas countryside.

The wagon, bigger than most bathrooms, is plumbed to go right into a septic system and has pipes to hook up to the ranch's hot- and cold-water system. It has copper screens to keep out the bugs and has been insulated and mouse-proofed.

WHAT TO LOOK FOR A sturdy undercarriage. If you're buying your first wagon, enlist the services of a local blacksmith or wheelwright.
WHAT TO AVOID A wagon that is rotted or, if tin covered, rusted.
WHAT IT'S GOING TO COST A vintage tar-paper shack wagon can cost from $50 to $500, depending on condition.
ON THE ROAD These wagons were built to be parked and only moved a few feet one way or the other, so they are best transported from place to place on a flatbed truck.

A portable bath house serves several guest wagons on Bee Young's Texas ranch, *above*. Elegance abounds with a deep claw-foot tub, antique furnishings, and fluffy towels, *opposite*. The stained-glass window swings open for unobstructed views of the countryside.

luxe cowgirl

MODEL: Foreman's sheep wagon
SIZE: 55 square feet
DESIGNERS: Hilary Heminway/Terry Baird
HOME BASE: Kalispell, Montana

*t*here is something so very charming about a restored sheep wagon that is cheerfully and comfortably decorated in natural fibers—wool, leather, and chintz. A clever combination of imagination and skill, and romance and practicality transforms a small, awkward space into a very livable one.

But when you acquire an antique wagon in a rough condition, you are still a long way from the romance of a sweet night's sleep in your own cozy little house.

According to designer Hilary Heminway, the first thing you will need to do when you buy an old wagon is get a dumpster and start tearing out the insides. Then comes the scrubbing and disinfecting. These wagons have seen many years (in some cases a hundred or more) of hard use. Sometimes they have sat vacant out on the sheep range for years before they are sold, so they will likely need a lot of elbow grease to make them habitable. Allow enough time to go through them thoroughly, throwing away anything that has been affected by rain, snow, dust, or mice.

When you're decorating your sheep wagon, remember that light colors and gauzy fabrics maximize space (paint a small space white to make it look larger), while dark colors and heavy fabrics make a space look small and cozy. Observing the correct scale is not always necessary. Too often we try to scale everything down, to miniaturize a small room's contents, in the belief

High-quality bedding and linens, along with a warm sheepskin blanket, turn a restored sheep wagon into a comfortable guest room, *opposite*. A vintage porcelain pail, *above*, is converted into a deep sink. A cute little cowgirl lamp, *below*, is perfect for reading Zane Grey novels late into the night.

A few inches of snow shouldn't ruin anyone's plans—a tightly built and weatherproofed sheep wagon can be as cozy in winter as it is in summer. Here the traditional layered-canvas top has been replaced with a wooden roof.

that small pieces of furniture and accessories will make a little space seem larger. On the contrary, filling a small room with small furniture will emphasize the small size of the room. Think big. Think comfortable.

One of the biggest worries of a sheep wagon owner is fire. Traditionally, the stove was vented through a pipe that came out of the canvas-covered roof or out the front of the wagon, right next to the door. It is precisely because of the danger of fire that Hilary advises owners not to put a stove in the wagon. Instead, make sure the wagon is built tight and is well-insulated and weather-proofed. This way it is possible to keep warm and sleep well under a luxurious down quilt or layers of attractive blankets.

WHAT TO LOOK FOR A wagon with reliable running gear. Watch the local newspapers in sheep-herding states like Wyoming, Montana, and Idaho for farm and ranch auctions.

WHAT TO AVOID Trailers with damage from water or mice will take much longer to restore. Trailers with fire damage should be avoided altogether. Broken running gear can be repaired but can cost $1,500 and up.

WHAT IT'S GOING TO COST Expect to pay $50-$2,500, depending on condition. If it doesn't have any structural damage, remodeling will run between $3,000 and "the sky's the limit."

REMODELING Tear out the old, the mildewed, and the mouse-damaged. Scrub and disinfect. Replace any rotting wood. Decorate boldly, using large furniture, hefty tables and hutches, and loads of pillows.

ON THE ROAD Antique wagons have steel-bound wooden wheels that are not road-worthy. By the 1920s, wagons were made with rubber wheels and a hitch so they could be moved by farm tractors and trucks.

Visit antiques shops and flea markets to pick up fun accessories for your sheep wagon. Look for western- and cowboy-themed pottery, spongeware, old spice tins, and mason jars. Old camping gear works well, too. Don't worry about matching—just buy what you like and let your personality shine through.

odds & ends

It wasn't all that long ago that having a big house—perhaps the biggest house—up on the hill was a measure of your wealth and status. If you had money, you spent it on building or buying a very large home that would make people sit up, take notice, and say "wow." Times have changed. People have changed. The very nature of wealth has changed. Small has become the new big.

The concept of habitation on a small, personal scale is being discussed in architectural circles. Some young architects, like Mike Latham and Lisa Hsieh, are working with fabric, Plexiglas, and acrylic to further explore the "intersections of architecture, art, and technology." Others, like Jennifer Siegal of the Office of Mobile Design, are creating innovatively designed homes using recycled and sustainable materials such as shipping containers, newspapers, and bamboo.

As cultures become increasingly global, new technologies are changing how we live at home, how we work, and how we travel. Nowhere is this more apparent than in Europe, where architects, artists, and designers have been experimenting with the entire concept of home. Dutch designer Dré Wapenaar makes tent structures for living, for birthing, or for dying. Adriaan Buekers, a professor of composite materials in the aerospace engineering department at the Delft University of Technology, is using lighter materials (like multilayered textiles strengthened by the addition of carbon-fiber resins) to make lighter-weight buildings. He envisions neighborhoods of portable, inflatable structures made with a minimum of material and maximum volume for optimal performance. Some of the new structures, like London architect Richard Horden's high-tech Ski Haus, take micro-architecture to a new level.

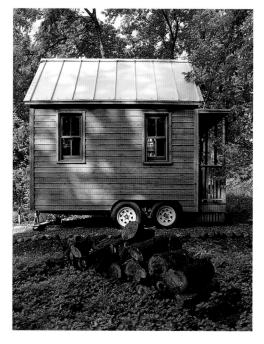

In a home where every square inch counts, the battery and fuse box for the solar charger and the water heater are hidden under the counter in the small (50 x 50 inch) kitchen. In cold weather, the propane stove warms the small house. When the house is stationary, *opposite*, Jay attaches a skirt and puts out steps. For travel, the additions tie down on the porch.

tiny tumbleweed

MODEL: Rolling gothic
SIZE: 144.5 square feet
OWNER: Jay Shafer
HOME BASE: Iowa City, Iowa

Jay was raised in a huge house and one of his (and his sister's) chores was vacuuming and dusting. "You could say that my affinity for tiny houses was born of my disdain for housekeeping," he says. "I just don't have the time or patience for the demands of a large house." Then, as an art student and later as a professor, he traveled to Japan, where land is so expensive that architects design small out of necessity. He was fascinated by how small his hotel room was, yet how comfortable.

When he started thinking about building his own home, he wanted something that met his needs without exceeding them and so began experimenting with size. "I designed, built, and now inhabit a house smaller than some people's bathrooms," says Jay.

The efficiencies he used were inspired not only by traditional Japanese design but by the clever use of space on boats and in trailers. He does away with transitional areas like hallways and stairwells and maximizes storage area. The Tumbleweed is one multipurpose, shipshape room with a sleeping loft above. He installed a gravity-fed shower, an under-counter refrigerator, a bar-sized sink, and a Dovre propane stove for heat and some minimal cooking. (He also has a portable double-burner propane stove bought in a camping store.)

Because it is rot- and bug-resistant as well as lightweight, he chose cedar for the outside of his home. On the inside, he used

An 18 x 12-inch table, *above,* is designed to fold up in the closet when not in use. Large closets and plenty of shelves provide storage and keep visual clutter at a minimum.

A sturdy ladder leads up to a comfortable sleeping loft with a full-sized bed and clothes closets. "There are only about four inches on each side of the bed," says Jay, "so making my bed is a challenge."

pine that he treated with several coats of boiled linseed oil—painted on and rubbed off several times because "it's not too shiny and gives the pine a good color."

"The uncomplicated, passive-solar design makes it easier to heat and cool," he says. Jay's heating bill comes to less than $30 worth of propane during a typical midwestern winter.

Building Tumbleweed took about 4,800 pounds of building materials and cost $42,000 (about one-fourth the cost of an average home). Just because the house is built smaller, it is not necessarily cheaper to build than a conventional house. At $400 per square foot, "my house is the cheapest house in Iowa City," says Jay, "but per square foot, it is the most expensive."

WHAT IT'S GOING TO COST Estimates for completed Tumbleweed homes (does not include the cost of site acquisition and development or the cost of moving the home): Rolling Gothic (125 square feet plus porch)—$39,000; Gothic Cross Gable (375 square feet plus porch)—$60,000; Two-bedroom Fat Bull's Eye (500 square feet plus porch)—$70,000. If you are a do-it-yourselfer, you can cut these costs in half by buying the plans from Tumbleweed Houses and building it yourself.

TIPS FOR FURNISHING Since each Tumbleweed is essentially one room with a sleeping loft above, it is important to buy or build multipurpose furniture. Jay's dining table doubles as a writing desk, and his heating stove can also be used for cooking. He also advises minimizing clutter by creating built-in bookcases, drawers, cupboards, and closets—and, of course, by simplifying your life.

ON THE ROAD Tumbleweed homes come with wheels and typically weigh 2,000 to 5,000 pounds. They can be pulled by a half-ton truck or SUV with a minimum of 200 horsepower.

in the woods

MODEL: Adirondack lean-to
SIZE: 96 square feet
OWNERS: Ken and Diane Pieper
HOME BASE: Evergreen, Colorado

Originating in the Adirondacks of upstate New York, lean-tos were built by nineteenth-century backcountry guides who needed a snug shelter while trekking through the woods. They often built these structures using only an axe.

Architectural designer Ken Pieper and his wife Diane used a few more tools but stayed true to the authentic Adirondack look and style. "We first saw an example of one while visiting the Adirondack Museum," says Ken. He and Diane loved the simple structure and brought back a small model. They followed the model as they built their own.

The lean-to is constructed of beetle-killed ponderosa pine and finished with a product called PeneTreat to repel insects; oakum chinking fills the cracks. The roof is hand-split Meeker cedar shakes.

CHOOSING FURNITURE   The small space of a lean-to instantly becomes cozy with warm, rugged materials and fabrics. The Piepers used Hudson Bay blankets and clothing. L.L. Bean and Early Winters also carry wonderful Adirondack-style bedding.

WHAT IT'S GOING TO COST   Ken and Diane spent between $6,000 and $7,000 to build and furnish their lean-to.

ON THE ROAD   The lean-to sits on a foundation of large rocks, which are left behind when the structure is moved. Pivoted on two large logs, the structure is simply hoisted onto a flatbed truck. Ken's lean-to measures 14 x 16 feet with the overhang, and moving it requires a permit except on the most rural of roads.

The tiny interior of this Adirondack-style lean-to, *opposite*, is warmed up with kerosene lamps and Hudson Bay bedding. The large overhang, *above*, keeps the interior protected from the elements.

The Carlson home was built out of four seagoing shipping containers—two steel-skinned and two aluminum.

packing-crate redux

MODEL: Carlson residence
SIZE: 3,000 square feet
DESIGNER: Office of Mobile Design
HOME BASE: Los Angeles, California

*j*ennifer Siegal is a Los Angeles-based architect whose designs were inspired by "an ongoing conversation with my grandfather, who sold hot dogs from a cart on Coney Island." Travels through Vietnam and Southeast Asia, where people not only "live smaller but find creative uses for things we would normally throw away" led Jennifer to experiment with creating buildings out of shipping containers and packing crates. She also uses other sustainable materials like recycled newspaper and bamboo. In 1998, she founded the Office of Mobile Design to create portable, high-quality, better-designed homes. "Although the Carlson house does not seem to be immediately mobile," she says, "we can take it apart and move the elements by road, train, or sea."

WHAT IT'S GOING TO COST Seagoing shipping containers run about $6,000 each. Converting one or more into a home can cost $200,000.
ON THE ROAD Shipping is via flatbed truck. Based on road width, the width of a shipping-container home can go up to thirteen feet. However, each home is based on a series of elements that get bolted together on-site.

High-output, roof-mounted solar panels charge two high-capacity batteries. The super-insulated camper shell reduces energy requirements.

roaming the earth

MODEL: EarthRoamer XV-LT
SIZE: 161 square feet
DESIGNERS: Michele Connolly
and Bill Swails/EarthRoamer.com
HOME BASE: Superior, Colorado

*N*ot just another RV, the EarthRoamer Expedition Vehicle is truck-mounted and environmentally friendly. It is totally self-contained and does not depend on external power or water hookups. Instead of propane, the EarthRoamer uses two solar-charged batteries to run most of the interior systems, including refrigerator, microwave oven, air conditioner, and a fifteen-inch flat-screen TV. The truck's 325-hp engine and the kitchen stove run on regular diesel or B20 biodiesel. The surprisingly roomy interior (6-foot-6-inch stand-up height) has a California king-sized over-cab bed.

JUST THE FACTS Built on a Ford F-450 chassis with a fiberglass body designed by a California boat builder, the EarthRoamer weighs 13,000 pounds and has two 255-amp/hour marine batteries powered by two 185-watt solar panels, a 6.0-cubic-foot compressor refrigerator/freezer, a 5,000-BTU air conditioner, a 100-gallon fresh-water supply with a dual fresh-water filtration system, a 25-gallon gray-water holding tank, a cassette toilet, and an enclosed bath/shower.
WHAT IT'S GOING TO COST $150,000. Gets between 11-15 mpg.

Dré Wapenaar describes himself as an artist who happens to work in tent design. "Tents are a gathering point for me."

among the trees

MODEL: Green tree tent
SIZE: 65 square feet
DESIGNER: Dré Wapenaar
HOME BASE: The Hersthoorn,
The Netherlands

*b*ecause it represents "our common home," Dutch sculptor Dré Wapenaar uses the tent as his artistic medium. The design of his tree tent developed itself "in a natural way" when he hung a circular floor up in a tree with a rope—form followed function. Dré made the outer skin of green cotton canvas supported by a steel frame. The resulting tree tent weighs about 440 pounds and is nine feet in diameter at the bottom, and twelve-feet high at the peak. Each tree tent is individually made. "I use design and architecture and work with constructors and engineers, but I'm still a sculptor," he says.

HOW TO HANG IT UP For safety reasons, Dré suggests hanging the tent relatively low on a sturdy tree. It is hoisted onto the tree with block and tackle belts at the upper "hanging point." For stability, Dré also connects the tent to the tree at two lower points.

ON THE ROAD If you don't dismantle the tent, you will need a full-sized pickup for transportation. If you dismantle the framework, the tent can be packed into a 12 x 4 x 2-foot crate.

The Hermit's Cabin is built of reclaimed barn wood from north Sweden. It is outfitted with everything necessary to live a "hermit's life."

like a hermit

MODEL: Hermit's Cabin
SIZE: 80 square feet
DESIGNERS: Mats Theselius, in collaboration with Arvesund Trädesign
HOME BASE: Mattmar, Sweden

designed and built by Swedish designer Mats Theselius, the Hermit's Cabin is fully equipped for one person. It is created from reclaimed barn wood from north Sweden. Mats describes the structure as an "escape from the intensity of urban life."

The cabin has won awards for its classically simple Scandinavian design and is being sold in an annual limited series of twenty-five cabins. It comes fully equipped with a bed, chair, table, wardrobe, and stove, or you can get just the shell and design your own interior.

WORKING WITH RECLAIMED WOOD Be sure to find a qualified, experienced dealer who can help you choose the right wood for the right project. Some popular woods are cypress, cedar, and heart pine.
WHAT TO AVOID Remember that reclaimed wood can be hundreds of years old; watch for insect infestation, excessive nails (they all have to be removed), and water or fire damage.
ON THE ROAD This home should be moved on a flatbed truck.

Making small, portable buildings is Richard Horden's profession as well as his hobby. His personal ski house is designed to be transported by helicopter.

high & light

MODEL: Ski Haus
SIZE: 140 square feet
DESIGNER: Richard Horden, Horden Cherry Lee, London
HOME BASE: Lauterbrunnen, Switzerland

*R*ichard Horden divides his time between London (where he has an architectural practice) and Munich (where he teaches at the Technical University). Because of his interest in ultralight, portable micro-buildings, he also works with NASA on aviation and space architecture.

JUST THE FACTS Ski Haus costs about $55,000 and is constructed of 2mm aluminum sheets with a light foam insulation. It weighs 661 pounds and sleeps four on bunk beds. Solar cells and a wind generator provide 12-volt power. Propane is used for heat and cooking in a tiny kitchen. A portable composting toilet can be carried underneath.
ON THE ROAD Ski Haus is aerodynamically designed to be moved from place to place by a small (Aerospaciale Lama) helicopter. It has three adjustable ice-axe legs for adapting to mountainous terrain.

Mike's box has a bed on top and doors that open to reveal well-designed living space. Lisa's box, *below,* can serve as an emergency shelter.

inside the box

MODEL: Home Box
SIZE: 36 square feet
DESIGNER: Mike Latham,
Arts.Corporation
HOME BASE: Brooklyn, New York

MODEL: Shelter Box
SIZE: 100 square feet
DESIGNERS: Lisa Hsieh with Jr-Gang Chi
HOME BASE:
New York,
New York

each year the prestigious Architectural League of New York (www.archleague.org) hosts a Young Architects Competition for architects or designers who have been out of school for ten years or less. The entries—theoretical or real—are judged by experienced members of the design community.

With a great deal of imagination, each of the young architects addresses the problem of compact, portable living—or living simply and lightly on the earth.

One of the winners, Mike Latham, designed a 6 x 6-foot steel-and-acrylic box that has been selling as a shelter and as a well-designed guest room or storage space. Mike's new company, Arts.Corporation, continues to explore the intersections of architecture, art, and technology. Lisa Hsieh designed a 10 x 10-foot module with aluminum structural beams (much like a tent) and an inflatable skin. The pod can be extended over a larger area or combined with other pods to create multiple spaces.

tools for the trip

Restoration Hardware (1) carries lots of fun, vintage-inspired products for your trailer, sheep wagon or tent: hand-crank radios, portable record players, compact telescopes, waterproof binoculars, and more. (800) 762-1005 or www.restorationhardware.com.

With a Global Positioning System (GPS), you'll never get lost. Several companies make them; find the one that's right for you. **Magellan** makes the SporTrak Topo, preloaded with 108 MB of interactive, nationwide topographic maps. (800) 707-9971 or www.magellangps.com.

For great dinnerware, look to **Marble Canyon** (2). From elegant to whimsical, these enamel-covered steel plates, with matching napkins and tablecloths, will have you dining like royalty no matter where you are. (505) 424-4940 or www.marblecanyon.org.

Every portable house needs a good first-aid kit. **Adventure Medical Kits** puts together comprehensive, easy-to-use kits in waterproof bags, covering everything from burns to fractures to stings. (800) 324-3517 or www.adventuremedicalkits.com.

Keep everything squeaky clean without harming the environment. **Vermont Soapworks** produces soaps, shower gels, non-toxic cleaners and even "camping soap" using all-natural, biodegradable ingredients. (866) 762-7482 or www.vtsoap.com.

Stay warm and snug on chilly nights with sleeping bags from **Slumberjack**. The Denali line features bags that range from -30 to 45 degrees. The company also offers portable furniture, shelters, and accessories, and the Web site offers lots of great travel tips. www.slumberjack.com.

For over 30 years, **Vasque** has provided top-quality boots for serious adventurers. Specializing in mountaineering, backpacking, and hiking boots, Vasque is sure to have the right boot for you. (800) 224-4453 or www.vasque.com.

Head out into the backcountry with the Mountain Safety Research Alpine Kitchen Set from the **Backcountry Store**. This clever kitchen includes squeeze bottles, salt and pepper/spice shakers, a plastic cutting board, and more. (800) 409-4502 or www.backcountrystore.com.

Always be in touch with the **Iridium System,** a satellite-based, wireless communications network. This system offers voice and data transmission to and from literally anywhere on earth. (866) 947-4348 or www.iridium.com.

1

2

Can't bear to give up your TV? With **Casio's** EV-680 portable TV, you won't have to. It has a three-inch color screen and runs for up to three hours on AA batteries. Casio has many toys for gadget lovers. (800) 836-8580 or www.casio.com.

Artist Michael Messenheimer uses common hardware products and machine parts to create funky table lights that work like flashlights (3). Available at **Sonrisa Furniture**, (800) 668-1020 or www.sonrisafurniture.com.

Enjoy a hot shower, even out in the middle of nowhere. **Solar Direct** offers a solar shower that you simply hook up to a water supply. Order from www.solardirect.com. **Zodi Outback Gear** has several models for RVs, camping, and hunting. (800) 589-2849 or www.zodi.com.

A leader in portable gear for over 100 years, **Coleman** (4) has everything you need to make traveling more comfortable and convenient, from lanterns to grills, tent lights to hot-water heaters. They even make a coffee pot that fits on your Coleman stove. (800) 835-3278 or www.coleman.com.

Like Airstreams? Then you'll love the Airstream Collection of furniture from **William Alan**. These sofas, chairs, and tables are as sleek and modern as the trailers that inspired them. (336) 885-6095 or www.williamalan.com.

Stay healthy and hydrated with the First Need Base Camp portable water purifier from **General Ecology**. It uses no chemicals, requires no electricity, and is certified to meed EPA Microbiological Purification Standards against cysts, bacteria, and viruses. (800) 441-8166 or www.generalecology.com.

Take great pictures, both panoramic and zoom, with the lightweight, portable XR AF28-300mm Ultra Zoom lense from **Tamron**. It fits Canon, Minolta, Nikon, and Pentax camera bodies. (631) 858-8400 or www.tamron.com.

Eat well on the road with all-natural, gourmet camping food from **Natural High**. Freeze-dried and dehydrated ingredients are used to create yummy and nutritious meals like eggs and bacon, chicken enchiladas, and fudge brownies. And with a shelf life of up to two years, you can stock up and travel far. (800) 423-3170 or www.naturalhigh.com.

Record the special moments of your journey in style with the Medioveo Leather Journal from **K. Schweizer**. Beautifully handcrafted in Italy, the 160-page journal features a gorgeous leather cover and acid-free, cotton rag paper. (800) 595-1688 or www.kschweizer.com.

Keep hardworking hands soft with Ranch Hand Cream from **The Cowgirl Company.** The all-natural ingredients are the best cure for dry, chapped hands. (888) 440-7549 or www.cowgirlenterprises.com.

3

4

91

trailers

Sites to see:

www.vintagecampers.com
www.vintage-vacations.com
www.airstream.net
www.tincantourists.com
www.spartantrailers.com

Stuff to read:

*Books: **Airstream: The History of the Land Yacht*** by Bryan Burkhart and David Hunt (Chronicle, 2000). ***Ready to Roll: A Celebration of the Classic American Travel Trailer*** by Arrol Gellner and Douglas Keister (Viking Press, 2003). ***The Sporting Road: Travels Across America in an Airstream Trailer*** by Jim Fergus (Griffin Trade, 2000). ***Travel Trailer: A Visual History of Mobile America*** by Bryan Burkhart, et al, (Gibbs Smith, 2002).

Magazines: **Lost Highways** (quarterly), www.losthighways.org; **Trailer Life** (monthly), www.trailerlife.com.

Other interesting info:

If you'd like to buy an Airstream Bambi (14 feet long) furnished down to the napkins and cutlery (also with hand-selected antiques and vintage pieces) and designed by Ralph Lauren, visit www.polo.com. The cost is $100,000 and the money benefits The Ralph Lauren Center for Cancer Care and Prevention.

SISTERS ON THE FLY

PAGES 10-15 www.sistersonthefly.com for information about buying and restoring vintage trailers—also a list of fly-fishing trips.

FAMILY, FRIENDS & FOOD

PAGES 16-19 Robert Sinskey Vineyards, Napa, CA, (800) 869-2030, www.wines.com. While traveling in the Spartan to organic farms along the Pacific coast, chef Maria Sinskey was inspired to write a cookbook **The Vineyard Kitchen** (Harper Collins, 2003).

FABERGÉ AIRSTREAM

PAGES 20-23 MacKenzie-Childs, Ltd., Aurora, NY, (888) 665-1999, www.mackenzie-childs.com. Victoria has begun restoring a 1907 ferryboat on which she and her husband plan to live.

COPPER CREEK TRAILER

PAGES 24-25 Montana Wagons, Hilary Heminway and Terry Baird, Big Timber, MT, (406) 932-6116 or (860) 535-3110. Montana Wagons also designs, builds, and furnishes sheep wagons and hard-sided tents.

buses & RVs

Sites to see:

www.busnut.com
www.mrsharkey.com
www.busconversions.com
www.bobsokol.com
www.classicvws.com
www.vvwca.com (Vintage Volkswagen Club of America)

Stuff to read:

Books: **The Bus Conversion Bible** by Dave Galey Bryan on the web at www.busnut.com. **Rolling Homes** by Jane Lidz (A&W Publishers, 1979). **The RV Handbook: Essential How-To Guide for the RV Owner** by Bill Estes (Trailer Life Books, 2001). **Select & Convert Your Bus into a Motorhome on a Shoestring** by Ben Rosander (self-published, 2002). **Shuttlebus and Van Conversions** by Dr. Carl Weisbrod. Available also on CD-ROM from www.wdslibrary.com. **VW Bus Custom Handbook** by Lawrence Meredith (Motorbooks International, 1994).

Magazines: **Conversion** (monthly), **Ultra VW** (monthly), **VW Trends** (monthly).

ROXANNE ROXANNE
PAGES 28-33 Page Hodel,
pagebox@aol.com.

SNUG BUG
PAGES 34-35 Randy Carlson,
TVA/old bug, Brea, CA, (714)
792-3975, www.oldbug.com.

ROCK-'N'-ROLL BUS
PAGES 36-37 Tom Martino,
Denver, CO,
www.troubleshooter.com.
European washer/dryer:
AEG/Zanussi, www.aeg.com.

*trains, planes
& boats*

Sites to see:
Trains:
To buy a private railroad car:
www.railmerchants.net.
To charter private railroad cars:
www.aaprco.com (American
Association of Private Railroad
Car Owners).
www.privaterailcars.net
www.trainweb.com
www.viarail.ca/privatecars (for
charters in Canada)
www.privatecarservice.net

Stuff to read:
Books: **The Streamline Era** by
Robert Reed (Golden West
Books, 2000). **The Streamlined
Decade** by Donald J. Bush
(G. Brazziler, 1975).
Magazines: **Private Varnish**
(bimonthly for private car
owners), pveditor@earthlink.net;
Railfan & Railroad (monthly),
www.railfan.com; **Rail Travel
News** (biweekly),
www.railtravelnews.com.

Other interesting info:
The American Association of Private
Railroad Car Owners offers more
than 50 cars in the U.S. and Canada
to charter by the day, week, or event
(like weddings or family reunions).

CARITAS
PAGES 40-41 Clark Johnson and
Nona Hill, (608) 850-3740,
www.highirontravel.com for information about chartering Caritas.

VIRGINIA CITY
PAGES 42-43 Wade and Julia Pellizzer, Redwood City, CA, (659)
369-6405, www.vcrail.com for
information about chartering
Virginia City.
Planes:
Sites to see: www.boeing.com
www.aso.com (aircraft
shopping online)
Stuff to read:
Books: **Executive Jets**
by Geza Szurovy.
Magazines: **Flying** (monthly),
www.flyingmag.com.

Other interesting info:
For information about fractional
ownership of a jet, log on to
www.netjets.com or
www.flexjet.com.

JET SET
PAGES 44-45 **Design team:**
Greenpoint Technologies,
Kirkland, WA, (425) 828-2777.
www.greenpnt.com.

Boats:
Sites to see:
to buy or restore a boat:
www.powerboat.com
www.woodenboatrepair.com
www.peaseboatworks.com
to charter a private boat:
www.classiccharters.com
www.woodenboatco.com

Stuff to read:

Books: **Wooden Boat Renovation: New Life for Old Boats Using Modern Methods** by Jim and Clint Trefethen (International Marine Publishing Co., 1993). **Yacht Style: Design and Decor Ideas for your Boat** by Daniel Spurr (International Marine/Ragged Mountain Press, 1997).

Magazines: **By-the-sea.com** (online), **Classic Boat** (monthly), **Wooden Boat** (bimonthly) www.woodenboat.com.

SECOND TIME AROUND

PAGES 46-49 Jack Fhillips Designs, Palm Beach, FL, (800) 656-4459.

tepees, tents & yurts

Sites to see:

www.whitebuffalolodges.com
www.neversummernordic.com

Stuff to read:

Books: **Circle Houses: Yurts, Tipis and Benders** by David Pearson (Chelsea Green, 2001). **Tipis & Yurts: Authentic Designs for Circular Shelters** by Blue Evening Star (Sterling, 1999). **Woodall Tenting Directory** (Woodall Publications, 2003).

RUSTIC CHIC

PAGES 52-55 Cassandra Lohr Design International, Inc., Boulder, CO, (303) 377-7121, www.cassandradesigns.com. To see Cassandra's rustic furniture designs, Egg & Dart, Ltd., Denver, CO. www.egg-and-dart.com.

BACK TO BASICS

PAGES 56-57 Sue Scott, to see Sue's designs in dinnerware and table lines, www.marblecanyon.org.

CANVAS CABIN

PAGES 58-61 Sandston's Shack-Up, Stephanie Sandston, Bozeman, MT, (406) 763-5588.

BACKCOUNTRY GETAWAY

PAGES 62-63 Colorado Yurt Company, Montrose, CO, (800) 288-3190 or (970) 240-2111. www.advancecanvas.com. *Other yurt companies:* Nesting Bird, Port Townsend, WA, (360) 385-3972, www.nestingbird.com; Pacific Yurts, Inc., Cottage Grove, OR, (800) 944-0240, www.yurts.com.

sheep wagons

Sites to see:

To buy a sheep wagon:
www.whitebuffalolodges.com
www.roadkingoutdoors.com
www.sheepwagon.com
To stay in a sheep wagon:
www.1880sranch.com
www.sheepwagonhideouts.com
www.usatouring.com
www.ravenwoodcastle.com

Stuff to read:

Books: **Sheepwagon: Home on the Range** by Nancy Weidel (High Plains Press, 2003).

AMERICAN GYPSY

PAGES 66-69 Ranch Willow Wagon Company, Lynn Arambel, Sheridan, WY, (307) 674-1510. Engel's Coach, Dave Engel, Joliet, Montana, (406) 962-3573, www.engelscoachshop.com. *Gypsy wagons from* Europe: gypsy-caravans.co.uk (vintage, fully restored, gypsy wagons).

BATH HOUSE

PAGES 70-71 Ranch Willow Wagon Company, Lynn Arambel, Sheridan, WY, (307) 674-1510.

LUXE COWGIRLS

PAGES 72-75 Montana Wagons, Hilary Heminway and Terry Baird, Big Timber, MT, (406) 932-6116 or (860) 535-3110.

odds & ends

Sites to see:
www.totemdesign.com
www.trukmate.com
www.doorsofperception.com
www.adirondacklean-tos.com

Stuff to read:
*Books: **Houses in Motion: The Genesis, History and Development of the Portable Building*** by Robert H. Kronenburg (Academy Editions, 2002). ***Lightness: Minimum Energy Structures*** by Adriaan Beukers (010 Publishers, 1998). ***Portable Architecture*** by Robert H. Kronenburg (Architectural Press, 2003). *Periodicals:* ***Environmental Building News*** (monthly) www.buildinggreen.com.

TINY TUMBLEWEED

PAGES 78-81 Jay Shafer, Iowa City, IA, (319) 936-6080, www.tumbleweedhouses.com.

IN THE WOODS

PAGES 82-83 Ken Pieper, Ken Pieper and Associates, Inc., Evergreen, CO, (303) 670-0619, www.kenpieper.com.

PACKING-CRATE REDUX

PAGE 84 Jennifer Siegal, Office of Mobile Design, Los Angeles, CA, (310) 439-2495, www.designmobile.com.

ROAMING THE EARTH

PAGE 85 Michele Connolly and Bill Swails, EarthRoamer.com, LLC, Superior, CO, (720) 304-3174, www.earthroamer.com.

AMONG THE TREES

PAGE 86 Created by Dré Wapenaar, Rotterdam, Netherlands, drewapenaar@zonnet.nl.

LIKE A HERMIT

PAGE 87 Designed by Mats Theselius for Arvesund Trädesign, Mattmar, Sweden, 011-46-640-44021, www.arvesund.se.

HIGH & LIGHT

PAGE 88 Richard Horden, Horden Cherry Lee Architects, London, UK, 011-44-207-495-4119, www.hcla.co.uk.

INSIDE THE BOX

PAGE 89 Steel-and-acrylic box, Mike Latham, Arts.Corporation, Brooklyn, NY, (718) 302-4164, www.artscorporation.com. Aluminum/inflatable box, Lisa Hsieh, (646) 495-7184.

Acknowledgements—*Many thanks to friends, neighbors, and, in some cases, total strangers (who, happily, have become friends) for sharing their portable house stories with us and allowing us to come in and photograph—sometimes on very short notice. Irene also wants to thank her dear David for love and support and joy. Mary wants to thank her family and friends—especially her handsome husband, Chris, and sons, Nick and Josh, who lived on frozen pizza and grilled cheese sandwiches for longer than they ever thought possible. Finally, we would like to thank our editor, Suzanne Taylor, who, with the patience of a near saint, encouraged and cajoled . . . and never once raised her voice.*

Photo Credits
Darrell T. Arndt: *pages 38, 43;* Povy Kendall Atchison: *pages 78, 79, 80, 81, 82, 83, 85;* Dona Kopol Bonick: *pages 26, 27;* Andrew Bordwin: *page 89 (large photos);* Randy Carlson: *pages 32, 33;* Carlos Domenech: *pages 46, 47, 48, 49;* Audrey Hall: *title page (small photo), pages 10-11, 12, 13, 14, 15, 24, 25, 58, 59, 60,-61, 64, 66-67, 68, 69, 70, 71, 72, 73, 74, 75, acknowledgements page;* Susanna Howe: *28, 29, 30, 31;* John Keuhl: *40, 41, 42;* David Marlowe: *title page (large photo), 50, 52, 53, 54-55, back cover;* Chris Marona: *cover (large photo), page 56, 57;* Lark Smotherman: *cover (small photo);* David Tsay: *contents page, pages 8, 16, 17, 18, 19.*

Photos on pages 20-23: *courtesy of Victoria MacKenzie-Childs;* photos on pages 44-45: *(interiors) courtesy of Rob Lancaster/Greenpoint Technologies, (exterior) courtesy of The Boeing Company;* photos on pages 62-63: *courtesy of Colorado Yurt Company;* photos on pages 76, 88: *courtesy of Richard Horden, Horden Cherry Lee;* photos on page 84: *courtesy of Office of Mobile Design;* photos on page 86: *courtesy of Dré Wapenaar;* photos on page 87: *courtesy of Arvesund Trädesign;* photo on page 89 (shelter box): *courtesy of Lisa Hsieh.*